Simply Delicious Maple Recipes

Simple Time Tested Recipes From The "Sugarin Farms" of Vermont

Margaret Sanborn

First Printing, 2012

Published by **ChefShane.com**

Printed in the United States of America

**For more great cooking pay us a visit at:
http://ChefShane.com**

Table of Contents

Preface

THE RECIPES in this book have been collected through the years from many different sources. They have been passed down from one generation to another and handed along from one friend to another, with revisions and changes in keeping with the times. All have been tested and edited carefully for accuracy. I only wish I knew the real source of every recipe so I could give full credit to the originator of each one.

A farm woman once said to me, "Almost any good recipe is better with maple sugar or syrup added." This statement may be a little far-fetched but it is true that the maple flavor is a real addition to many favorite dishes.

I hope that looking at the charming pictures of old-fashioned sugaring and making some of these delicious old maple dishes may conjure up for you a little of the gala "sugarin' off" feeling that means so much to all of us who grew up in the country.

M. S.

The Sugar Maple

THERE'S A STORY that an Indian squaw was the first to discover the sweetness of maple sap. She was cooking a rabbit or a piece of venison one day and, for lack of water, she caught some of the sap that was running freely from an opening in a maple tree. She cooked the meat in this, and it made such a hit with her menfolks that they decided to tap some more trees.

Whether this is truth or fiction, we do know that the Indians probably used their tomahawks to make a diagonal incision in the trunk of the maple. In this they inserted a reed, or a concave piece of bark, through which the sap was conveyed to a bark trough.

The early white settlers substituted wooden spouts for the bark and used copper or iron kettles for boiling the sap down. They hung the kettles on poles and boiled the sap over fires made from green wood which they cut as needed. Next came the pot-ash kettle supported by two crotched posts. A few years later, sheet iron pans were set on stone fire-places built in the woods.

Much later, sugar houses with chimneys were built with regular arches for the pans. In time, evapora-tors were invented, vats or storing tubs were built for holding the sap, and teams of horses replaced the oxen for hauling the sap to the place where it was boiled.

Today, pipe lines carry the sap to the sugar house, and many new inventions have simplified the whole process of maple sugar making. But to anyone with a bit of Vermont blood in his veins, "sugarin' time" means getting together for a sugar party in the woods — the ultimate in good food and good companionship.

From the first of March to the middle of April, as winter breaks into the warm days of spring, you'll hear farmers saying, "Guess the sap will run today!" And, after gathering the sap and boiling it down, there'll be a "sugarin' off." Slabs of homemade bread, dill pickles, dozens of raised doughnuts and baked ham, with eggs boiled in the sap, are part of the feast. The main dish, however, is sugar on snow — golden syrup cooked just enough to set in little pools on hard packed snow and then popped into the mouth.

Sap cooked down to a syrup consistency is sold as Maple Syrup. Cooked longer, it becomes Maple Sugar and is sold as such in tin cans or tin pails. If beaten to a smooth consistency, it is known as Maple Cream. Of course, a great amount of the maple product you see in the markets is a processed candy.

Sugar on Snow

Either maple syrup or maple sugar may be used for this. If syrup is used, boil it until, when dropped on well-packed snow from the tip of a spoon, it remains waxy. Then spread it in "bite-sized" pools on the surface of the snow or on a block of ice.

If maple sugar is used, add a little water and melt it carefully to prevent burning. Then proceed in manner given above.

Whether you use syrup or sugar, this is one of the most delicious treats you can have. No out-of-state guest should ever leave without having sugar on snow — even if he has to have it "on ice."

Suggestions for Storing Maple Syrup and Sugar

SYRUP should be stored in a dry, cool place. For family use, the smaller containers — quarts and half gallons — are recommended. If syrup is purchased in gallons, it is wise to remove it from the can, heat it to the boiling point, and seal it up hot in glass fruit jars with new rubbers. In this way it keeps well for a long time. If maple syrup should ferment slightly, it may be restored to its normal flavor by heating it to the boiling point and then skimming it.

SUGAR should also be stored in a cool, dry place. If stored in a tightly covered tin, it is apt to mold and ferment on top. To prevent this, take off the tin cover and paste a piece of manila paper tightly over the top.

Recipe Notes

If a recipe calls for maple sugar and you have only maple syrup on hand, simply boil the syrup slowly until it threads. Remove from fire and beat until thick.

On the other hand, if a recipe calls for maple syrup and you have only maple sugar, simply add a small amount of water to the sugar and cook very slowly until sugar is entirely melted and mixture is of the consistency of syrup.

Throughout this book, when the word "sugar" is used in a recipe, it refers to granulated or white sugar. If maple, brown or confectioner's sugar is indicated, it is so stated.

Some of the older recipes use terms or ingredients which may not be familiar to modern readers. So where possible, I have added notes explaining process or substitutions that may be used.

Oven Temperatures

Many old recipes list oven temperatures as moderate oven, hot oven, fast oven, etc. instead of giving you actual temperatures. In this book, the oven temperatures in Fahrenheit are also included. Here is a chart for reference.

Table of equivalent oven temperatures

Description	°F	°C
Cool Oven	200°F	90°C
Very Slow Oven	250°F	120°C
Slow Oven	300-325°F	150-160°C
Moderately Slow	325-350°F	160-180°C
Moderate Oven	350-375°F	180-190°C
Moderately Hot	375-400°F	190-200°C
Hot Oven	400-450°F	200-230°C
Very Hot Oven	450-500°F	230-260°C
Fast Oven	450-500°F	230-260°C

Nutritional Information

Nutritional value per 100 g (3.5 oz) Maple Syrup	
Energy	260 calories
Carbohydrates	67.09 g
Sugars	59.53 g
Dietary fiber	0 g
Fat	0.20 g
Protein	0 g
Thiamine (B1)	0.006 mg (1%)
Riboflavin (B2)	0.01 mg (1%)
Niacin (B3)	0.03 mg (0%)
Pantothenic acid (B5)	0.036 mg (1%)
Vitamin B6	0.002 mg (0%)
Calcium	67 mg (7%)
Iron	1.20 mg (9%)
Magnesium	14 mg (4%)
Manganese	3.298 mg (157%)
Phosphorus	2 mg (0%)
Potassium	204 mg (4%)
Zinc	4.16 mg (44%)

Source: USDA Nutrient Database

Percentages are relative to US recommendations for adults.

Bread & Rolls

Maple Muffins

Here's a special breakfast treat — delicious with crisp bacon and hot coffee.

2 cups flour
3 teaspoons baking powder
1/2 teaspoon salt
1/2 cup soft maple sugar
1 cup milk
1 large egg
4 tablespoons melted fat

Mix and sift flour, baking powder, and salt. Add maple sugar, milk, and beaten egg. Beat well and fold in melted fat. Place in greased muffin tins and bake 15 to 20 minutes in oven (375°F).

Makes eighteen 2 1/2-inch muffins.

Maple Butternut Biscuits

2 cups flour
4 teaspoons baking powder
1 teaspoon salt
2 tablespoons shortening
3/3 cup milk

Filling:
1 cup soft maple sugar
1/4 cup cream
1/2 cup chopped butternut meats

Mix and sift dry ingredients. Cut shortening in with a knife, add milk, toss on floured board and roll lightly to 1/2-inch thickness. Combine maple sugar, cream, and butternut meats, and spread over dough. Roll like jelly roll, slice, place on greased cookie sheet, and bake 20 minutes at 400°F.

Makes 18 biscuits.

Maple Biscuits I

These dress up the simplest supper.

2 cups flour
4 teaspoons baking powder
1/2 teaspoon salt
2 tablespoons shortening
3/4 cup milk
1 cup soft maple sugar

Sift dry ingredients together and cut in shortening. Add milk and roll on floured board to 3/4-inch thickness. Spread with maple sugar, roll like jelly roll. Slice and bake on greased tin in oven (375°F) for 15 minutes.

Makes 18 biscuits.

Fun Fact:
Three-quarters of the world's supply of maple syrup comes from the Canadian province of Quebec.

Maple Biscuits II

2 cups flour
4 teaspoons baking powder
1/2 teaspoon salt
4 tablespoons butter or other shortening
3/4 cup milk
Grated maple sugar

Sift the dry ingredients together. Add the butter, working in with a fork. Add the milk to make a soft dough. Place on a floured board and toss lightly until the outer surface looks smooth. Roll out one-half inch thick and cut with floured biscuit cutter. Place them on a greased baking pan, brush the tops of the biscuits with melted butter and sprinkle generously with grated maple sugar. Bake in a hot oven, 425°F, for about 12 minutes.

Bran Bread

1 1/2 cups flour
3 teaspoons baking powder
1 level teaspoon salt
1/4 cup sugar
1 1/2 cups bran
1/2 cup dates, chopped
1 egg
3/4 cup milk
1/2 cup maple syrup
4 tablespoons melted shortening

Mix and sift flour, baking powder, salt, and sugar. Add remaining ingredients in order given. Mix well. Pour into 8 by 4 inch greased loaf pan. Bake about 50 minutes in moderate oven, (350°F).

Nut Brown Bread

2 cups flour
4 teaspoons baking powder
1 teaspoon salt
3/4 cup milk
4 tablespoons maple syrup
1 egg
1 cup chopped nuts or raisins

Sift dry ingredients together, add milk, syrup and beaten egg. Add chopped nuts or raisins. Pour into greased bread tin and bake 1 hour in oven, (350°F).

Fun Fact:
In the 16th and 17th centuries, processed maple sap was the main source of sugar. Cane sugar was much more expensive, as it had to be imported from the West Indies.

Quick Maple Bread

1 cup flour
2 cups whole wheat flour
1/2 cup maple sugar
2 cups sour milk
1 1/2 teaspoons soda
1 teaspoon salt

Sift flour, add maple sugar. Mix sour milk, soda, and salt, and add to first mixture. Mix thoroughly, pour into greased bread tin, and bake 1 hour in moderate oven (350°F).

Note: Many old recipes call for sour milk. Back then it was likely they used milk that was left sitting out. These days, there is an easier way to get the sour milk you need for your favorite recipe. Start with 1 cup of milk. Whole or 2% is ideal for baking. Add 1 teaspoon lemon juice or plain white vinegar. Stir together and let sit for 10-15 minutes. You should see a slight curdling. Your sour milk is ready for baking. While not quite the same cultured buttermilk from your grocery store also makes a satisfactory substitute for sour milk.

Maltex Raised Bread

(Quick Method)

3 cups flour
3/3 cup Maltex Cereal
1 1/2 yeast cakes
3 tablespoons lukewarm water
1 cup lukewarm milk
2 tablespoons maple syrup
1 1/2 teaspoons salt
3 tablespoons melted shortening

Sift flour into a bowl, add Maltex Cereal. Dissolve yeast cakes in lukewarm water and add to lukewarm milk, syrup and salt. Combine this liquid with flour and Maltex and add melted shortening. Knead the dough until smooth and let stand in warm place for 30 minutes. Cut down, knead well and shape into loaf. Place in greased 5x10 inch pan and let stand to rise about 45 minutes. Bake 45 minutes in oven at 375°F.

Note: Maltex is an old fashioned hot cereal which has been around since 1899! Looks to be a blend of toasted wheat and malted barley syrup. This is nothing I have ever seen in stores. The brand has changed hands a few times over the years. Surprisingly, it is still manufactured by a company called Homestat Farm in Pennsylvania. http://www.homestatfarm.com/. I'm guessing it is pretty similar to Malt-O-Meal or Cream of Wheat.

Corn Bread

1 cup corn meal
1 1/4 cups flour
1 1/2 teaspoons baking powder
1 teaspoon salt
3/4 teaspoon soda
4 tablespoons maple syrup
1 egg, well beaten
1 1/4 cups sour milk
3 tablespoons melted shortening

Sift dry ingredients together. Add syrup, egg, sour milk and shortening. Mix well and bake in 10-inch greased pun in moderate oven (350°F) about 40 minutes.

Cakes & Cookies

Maple Syrup Cake

1/3 cup shortening
1/2 cup sugar
3/4 cup maple syrup
1/3 cup milk
2 1/4 cups flour
1/2 teaspoon salt
3 teaspoons baking powder
3 egg whites
1 teaspoon vanilla

Cream the shortening and sugar. Add syrup and stir. Add milk alternately with flour, salt, and baking powder, mixed and sifted together. Fold in the beaten egg whites, add vanilla and bake in greased oblong pan about 9 inches by 4 inches. Bake 35 minutes at 350°F.

Maple Sugar Cake

1 1/4 cups flour
1/2 teaspoon salt
2 teaspoons baking powder
1 egg yolk
3/4 cup maple sugar
1 tablespoon shortening
6 tablespoons milk
1 teaspoon vanilla

Mix and sift dry ingredients. Beat egg yolk, sugar, and shortening together. Add milk, then combine all ingredients and beat well. Bake in a greased 8-inch square pan in a moderate oven (350°F) for 25 minutes. Use egg white for icing.

Fun Fact:
The most prevalent sugar in maple syrup is sucrose with small amounts of other sugars.

Maple Nut Cake

This is a very rich cake that keeps well.

1/2 cup shortening
1 cup maple sugar
2 eggs
1/2 cup milk
2 cups flour
3 teaspoons baking powder
1/2 teaspoon salt
1 teaspoon vanilla
1 cup chopped butternut meats
1 cup chopped seedless raisins

Cream the shortening; add the sugar and the well-beaten eggs. Add the milk alternately with the flour which has been mixed and sifted with the baking powder and salt. Add the vanilla, chopped nut meats, and chopped raisins. Mix thoroughly and place in a 10-inch square tin, which has been greased and floured. Bake 35-40 minutes in moderate oven (350°F).

Maple Tea Cakes

For the Ladies' Aid Tea.

1/3 cup shortening
1/4 cup sugar
1 cup maple sugar shavings
1 egg, well beaten
1/2 cup milk
2 cups flour
3 teaspoons baking powder
1/2 teaspoon salt
1/2 cup finely chopped nuts

Cream the shortening with the sugar and maple sugar shavings. Add the well beaten egg and milk. Add flour mixed and sifted with the baking powder and salt. Add the chopped nuts and mix well. Place in small greased muffin tins and bake 10-12 minutes in moderate oven (350°F).

Makes twenty-four 1 inch cakes.

Boiled Maple Cake

2/3 cup maple sugar
         or
1 cup maple syrup
1/2 cup melted shortening
1 teaspoon each cloves, nutmeg, cinnamon, salt
1 cup seedless raisins
1 cup cold water

Boil above ingredients together for 4 minutes after boiling begins. Chill thoroughly, then add:

2 cups flour sifted with
1 teaspoon soda

Add:
1/2 cup chopped nut meats

Beat well and bake in loaf tin in moderate oven (350°F) for about 1 hour.

Maple Gingerbread I

This is the kind Mother used to make.

2 cups flour
1/2 teaspoon salt
1 teaspoon soda
1 teaspoon ginger
1 egg
1 cup sour cream
1 cup maple syrup

Mix and sift dry ingredients. Beat egg well and mix with sour cream and syrup. Combine these two mixtures, stir, and turn into greased cake pan 9 inches square. Bake 25-30 minutes in oven (350°F).

Serve with whipped cream as a dessert, or with butter as a hot bread.

Fun Fact:
It takes between 5 and 13 gallons of maple sap to make 1 quart of maple syrup.

Maple Gingerbread II

1/4 cup shortening
1/2 cup maple syrup
1/2 cup brown sugar
3/4 cup sour milk
2 eggs
2 cups flour
1 teaspoon ginger
1 teaspoon soda
1/4 teaspoon salt

Heat shortening, syrup, and sugar together in a saucepan Add sour milk and beaten eggs. Add dry ingredients, mixed and sifted together. Mix well, place in greased 9-inch square cake pan. Bake at 350°F for 25-30 minutes.

Maple Upside Down Cake

3 tablespoons butter
1 cup maple sugar
1 cup pineapple sections
3 eggs
1 cup sugar
1/4 cup milk
1 teaspoon lemon extract
1 cup flour
1/2 teaspoon salt
1 1/2 teaspoons baking powder

Melt butter in bottom of 8 inch round cake pan. Mix in maple sugar and arrange pineapple sections to cover bottom of pan. Make cake mixture, mixing beaten egg yolks with sugar, then adding milk and flavoring, then flour, salt, and baking powder, mixed and sifted together. Fold in stiffly beaten egg whites, and pour this batter over mixture in cake pan. Bake 45 minutes at 350°F. Invert on large plate and serve with whipped cream.

Sour Cream Cake

One of the wonderful ways to use sour cream you have saved.

1 egg
1 1/2 cups flour
1 cup maple sugar
1 teaspoon soda
1 cup thick sour cream
1/2 teaspoon salt
1 teaspoon vanilla

Beat egg thoroughly, add sugar, and continue beating. Add sour cream alternately with flour which has been mixed and sifted with soda and salt. Add flavoring, stir well, and turn into greased 9-inch square cake pan. Bake in oven at 350°F for 25-30 minutes.

This may be served plain or with the icings given later in this book.

Quick Spice Cake

1/2 cup shortening
3/4 cup sugar
1/4 cup maple syrup
2 eggs
1/3 cup milk
1 3/4 cup flour
2 teaspoons baking powder
1/2 teaspoon salt
1/2 teaspoon cinnamon
1/4 teaspoon cloves
1 teaspoon vanilla

Cream shortening, add sugar, syrup, and beaten eggs, and blend well. Add milk, then dry ingredients, mixed and sifted, and then vanilla. Beat well and bake in greased to inch square cake pan in moderate oven (350°F) about 40 minutes.

Frost with maple hard sauce icing.

Maple Syrup Cookies

Keep these on hand in the cookie jar. They're "nice to come home to."

1 cup maple syrup
1/2 cup soft butter
2 eggs
1 teaspoon vanilla
1/2 cup milk
3 cups flour
1 teaspoon baking powder
1/4 teaspoon salt

Beat syrup and butter to a cream. Add eggs, well beaten, and vanilla. Add milk alternately with flour mixed and sifted with baking powder and salt. Roll lightly on floured board to 1/8 inch thickness, and cut with cookie cutter. Place on greased cookie sheets and bake 10-12 minutes in oven (400°F).

Makes 4 dozen 2-inch cookies.

Oatmeal Maple Syrup Drop Cookies

1/2 cup shortening
1 cup maple syrup
1 egg, beaten
1 1/2 cups flour
1 teaspoon salt
2 teaspoons baking powder
1/4 cup milk
1/2 cup seedless raisins
1 1/2 cups oatmeal
1/2 cup chopped nut meats

Beat shortening, maple syrup, and egg. Sift together flour, salt, baking powder. Add to first mixture alternately with milk. Mix well. Add raisins, oatmeal and nuts. Drop by spoonful on greased cookie sheet. Bake at 375°F about 15 minutes.

Makes 4 dozen cookies.

Rolled Maple Sugar Cookies

1 cup shortening
2 tablespoons milk
3/4 cup maple sugar
4 cups flour
1 cup sugar
2 teaspoons baking powder
2 eggs, well beaten
1/2 teaspoon salt
2 teaspoons vanilla or maple flavoring

Cream shortening with sugars. Add well-beaten eggs, milk, and vanilla. Add flour, baking powder, and salt, sifted together. Mix and chill thoroughly. Roll out thin on floured board and cut with cookie cutter. Bake on greased cookie sheets in quick oven, (450°F), for 10 minutes.

Makes 6 dozen 3-inch cookies.

Butterscotch Squares

1/4 cup butter or margarine
1 teaspoon baking powder
1 cup maple sugar
1/4 teaspoon salt
1 egg
1 teaspoon vanilla
1 cup flour
1/2 cup chopped nut meats

Cream butter and sugar. Add egg, flour, baking powder, salt and vanilla. Mix well, and stir in nut meats. Spread in 9-inch cake pan. Bake at 350°F until done. Cut in squares while still warm.

Fun Fact:
Maple sap is collected at the start of the spring thaw, usually in March and April. Weather conditions determine how long the "sugaring season" lasts. Warmer weather changes the consistency of the sap and makes it unsuitable for sugaring. Seasons typically last 4 to 8 weeks.

Cornflake Cookies

1/2 cup shortening
3/4 cup maple sugar
1 egg
3 tablespoons milk
1 teaspoon vanilla
1 1/4 cups flour
1/2 teaspoon soda
1 1/4 cups cornflakes
1/2 cup chopped dates or raisins

Cream shortening, sugar and beaten egg. Add milk and vanilla, then flour and soda, mixed and sifted together. Stir in cornflakes and dates or raisins. Drop from teaspoon on greased cookie sheets and bake 12-15 minutes at 350°F.

Makes 4 dozen 2-inch cookies.

Ginger Snaps

This is a very old recipe. These cookies, used to be kept on hand in a stone crock and eaten by the dozen, with milk, for the evening snack.

1/2 cup shortening
1 cup maple sugar
1 egg
1/2 cup sour cream
1/2 teaspoon soda
1 teaspoon ginger
Flour to make stiff dough

Cream shortening and maple sugar. Add beaten egg. Mix soda and ginger with sour cream and add to first mixture. Add flour and blend thoroughly. Roll very thin on floured board. Cut and bake on greased cookie sheet 8-10 minutes in oven at 450°F.

Makes 3 dozen 3-inch cookies.

Maple Kisses

1 cup maple sugar
1/4 teaspoon cream of tartar
1/2 cup brown sugar
6 marshmallows
1/2 cup water
1 egg white

Boil sugars, water and cream of tartar in saucepan until it becomes brittle when dropped in cold water from tip of spoon. Then add marshmallows, cut in pieces, and let stand 5 minutes. When melted, pour over stiffly beaten egg white. Beat until light. Drop from teaspoon on waxed paper. Garnish each piece with candied cherry or pecan meat.

Makes 30 kisses.

Peanut Butter Cookies

3 tablespoons shortening
1 cup maple sugar
1 egg, well beaten
3 tablespoons sour cream
1 1/2 cups flour
1 teaspoon soda
1/2 teaspoon salt
1/2 cup peanut butter

Cream shortening with maple sugar. Add well-beaten egg and sour cream. Add flour mixed and sifted with soda and salt. Add peanut butter and mix well. Roll small pieces of dough, about the size of a walnut, between palms of hands and place on greased tin. Criss cross with fork. Bake 10-15 minutes in hot oven (450°F).

Makes 36 two-inch cookies.

Maple Meringue Cookies

1/4 cup butter or margarine
1/2 cup sugar
1 egg, separated
3/4 cup flour
1/2 teaspoon baking powder
1/4 teaspoon salt
1 teaspoon vanilla or maple flavoring
1/2 cup chopped walnut meats
1 cup maple sugar

Cream butter and sugar, add egg yolk beaten, then flour mixed and sifted with baking powder and salt. Add flavoring. Spread to 1/4-inch thickness in greased 10-inch cake pan. Sprinkle with nut meats. Cover with meringue made by beating egg white until stiff and folding in maple sugar. Bake 30 minutes at 350 F. Cut in squares to serve.

Pies

Basic Pie Pastry

Here is a great basic pie pastry recipe you can use with the following pie recipes.

2 cups all purpose flour
1/2 tsp salt
3/4 cup Crisco
5-6 tbsp cold water

Combine the flour and salt in a medium mixing bowl. Cut in Crisco with a pastry blender until mixture resembles coarse meal. Sprinkle water evenly over surface; stir with a fork until dry ingredients are moistened. Shape dough into a ball until smooth.

Note: Do not overwork the dough because you will lose your nice flaky crust. This is the leading cause of hard, unappetizing pie crusts.

This recipe makes enough dough for one 9 or 10-inch double crust pie.

Maple Chiffon Pie

1 tablespoon gelatine
3 tablespoons cold water
1/2 cup milk
1/2 cup maple syrup
1/3 teaspoon salt
2 eggs, separated
1 cup thick cream
1 teaspoon vanilla

Soak gelatine in cold water. Heat milk, maple syrup, and salt in top of double boiler, and pour slowly over beaten egg yolks. Return to double boiler, add soaked gelatine and cook until it thickens. Chill and then fold in stiffly beaten egg whites and 1/2 of cream whipped and vanilla. Pour into baked 9-inch pie shell. Chill and top with remaining whipped cream.

Fun Fact:
The largest producer of maple syrup in the United States is Vermont. New York and Maine are also major producers. Smaller quantities are also produced in Wisconsin, Ohio, New Hampshire, Michigan, Pennsylvania, Massachusetts, and Connecticut.

Unsweetened Apple Pie

(with Maple Sauce)

This is one of the oldest maple recipes.

6 apples
Pastry for 1 crust
1 cup maple syrup
2 egg whites

Slice apples into buttered deep pie plate. Cover with pastry and bake 40 minutes at 375°F (or until apples are soft).

Serve warm with sauce made by cooking maple syrup until it just begins to thread, then pouring it slowly into beaten egg whites and beating it slightly.

Maple Sugar Pie (Two Crust) I

1 egg
1 tablespoon soft butter
1 cup soft maple sugar
1 tablespoon flour
1 cup thin cream or top milk

Beat egg and blend with maple sugar, butter, flour
and cream. Line an 8-inch pie plate with pastry and
pour the above mixture into it. Cover with top crust
and bake at 350° F for 45 minutes.

Note: Top milk is the upper layer of milk after the
top layer of cream has already been skimmed off.
Being that most of us no longer get our milk fresh
from the farm anymore a good modern substitute
might be light cream or even half and half.

Maple Sugar Pie (Two Crust) II

1 cup scraped maple sugar
1 1/4 cups milk
1 tablespoon flour or cornstarch
1 egg
2 tablespoons butter
1/4 teaspoon salt
1/4 teaspoon nutmeg

Heat maple sugar and milk in top of double boiler. Mix flour or cornstarch, egg, butter, salt and nutmeg, and stir into heated milk. Cook until thick and creamy, stirring constantly. Use as filling in a two-crust, 9-inch pie. Bake 40 minutes at 375°F.

Maple Sugar Pie (One Crust)

2 egg yolks
1 cup maple sugar
1 tablespoon flour
1/4 teaspoon salt
1 tablespoon soft butter
2 cups milk
1 teaspoon vanilla

Meringue:
2 egg whites
4 tablespoons sugar

Blend egg yolks, maple sugar, flour, salt and soft butter. Add milk and cook in top of double boiler until thick, stirring constantly. Remove from flame, add vanilla. Pour into baked 9-inch crust and cover with meringue made from stiffly beaten egg whites and sugar. Bake in slow oven (325°F) until meringue is golden brown.

Butternut Cream Pie (One Crust)

2 egg yolks
1 cup maple sugar
1 teaspoon flour
2/3 cup sour cream
1/8 teaspoon soda
1/4 teaspoon salt
1 cup butternut meats

Meringue:
2 egg whites
4 tablespoons sugar
1 teaspoon vanilla

Mix beaten egg yolks with sugar and flour. Add sour cream in which soda and salt have been dissolved. Mix well and add whole butternut meats. Pour into 9-inch unbaked pie shell and bake in oven at 350°F until thick. Cover with meringue made from stiffly beaten egg whites, sugar, and vanilla. Brown in oven at 325°F.

Old Fashioned Sugar Pie

1 1/2 cups maple sugar
1/8 teaspoon nutmeg
2 tablespoons butter
2/3 cup thick cream

Line a pie plate with pastry. Fill with maple sugar. Dot with butter and sprinkle with nutmeg. Pour cream over this. Put strips of pastry over the top in lattice work and bake in 375°F oven until sugar is melted.

Squash Pie

1 cup steamed squash, strained
3/4 cup maple syrup
2 eggs
1/2 teaspoon salt
1/2 teaspoon ginger
3/4 teaspoon cinnamon
1 cup top milk

Mix in order given. Fill unbaked 8-inch pie shell. Bake at 450°F for 10 minutes and at 350°F for 40 minutes.

Maple Custard Pie

A favorite with Vermonters who know their pies.

3 cups milk
1/4 cup sugar
3 eggs, separated
1 tablespoon flour
1 cup maple syrup
1/4 teaspoon salt
1 teaspoon vanilla

Scald milk and add to it the well-beaten yolks of eggs mixed with the maple syrup, sugar, flour, and salt. Continue cooking, stirring constantly, until it begins to thicken slightly. Then fold in the stiffly beaten whites and vanilla. Pour into uncooked 10-inch pie shell and bake in moderate oven (325°F) until firm.

Serves 6 people.

Maple Apple Pie

6 apples
1/2 teaspoon cinnamon
1 cup maple sugar
1 tablespoon butter
2/3 cup thick cream

Pare, core and slice apples, and arrange on an 8-inch pie crust, uncooked. Sprinkle with maple sugar and cinnamon and dot with butter. Pour the cream over this. Bake in 450°F oven 10 minutes, reduce to 350°F and bake until the apples are soft.

Pork Apple Pie

6 large apples
1/8 teaspoon black pepper
1 cup maple sugar
1 teaspoon cinnamon
1/2 pound fat salt pork

Pare apples and slice very thin. Mix thoroughly with sugar, pepper and cinnamon. Arrange apples in 10-inch pastry shell and cover top with very thin strips of salt pork. Add top crust and bake for 45 minutes at 350°F.

Deep Dish Apple Pie

6 apples
1 cup soft maple sugar
2 tablespoons flour
1/2 teaspoon cinnamon
1/2 teaspoon salt
1 tablespoon butter

Pare apples and slice very thin, add maple sugar, flour mixed with cinnamon and salt. Place in deep buttered casserole, dot with butter, and cover with rich pastry mixture. Bake in moderate oven (375°F) for 1 hour. Serve hot with thin cream poured over the top.

Makes 6 servings.

Pumpkin Pie

A deluxe version of an old favorite.

2 cups steamed pumpkin
1/2 teaspoon cinnamon
2 egg yolks
2 cups cream
2/3 cup maple sugar
1 teaspoon vanilla
1/2 teaspoon ginger
1/2 teaspoon salt
2 egg whites

Mix ingredients in order given, folding beaten egg whites in last. Place in 10-inch uncooked pie shell and bake at 350°F for 45 minutes.

Fun Fact:
Maple syrup is rich in potassium, calcium, manganese, and zinc.

Desserts

Maple Cream Pudding

Children will love this.

2 eggs, separated
3/4 cup maple syrup
2 tablespoons cornstarch
1/4 teaspoon salt
2 cups milk
1 teaspoon vanilla

Place egg yolks in top of double boiler and beat slightly. Add maple syrup, cornstarch and salt. Add milk and cook until thick, stirring constantly. Remove from flame and cool. Fold in stiffly beaten egg whites and chill. Top with whipped cream.

Makes 6 servings.

Maple Rice Pudding

3 eggs
1 cup maple sugar
2 cups milk
2 cups boiled rice
1/2 teaspoon salt
1/2 teaspoon nutmeg
1 cup raisins

Beat eggs slightly. Add maple sugar, milk, rice, salt, nutmeg and raisins. Bake at 350°F in buttered baking dish until firm. Serve with thin cream.

This serves 6 people.

Fun Fact:
Sugar maples, Red maples, and Black maples are the most common trees that sap is collected from for making maple syrup.

Maple Butternut Pudding

2 tablespoons sugar
1/4 cup flour
1/4 teaspoon salt
2/3 cup maple syrup
2 eggs, well beaten
1 1/2 cups milk
1 tablespoon butter
1 teaspoon vanilla
1/3 cup chopped butternut meats

Blend sugar, flour and salt. Add syrup and eggs and heat in top of double boiler. Add milk and cook slowly, stirring constantly, until thick. Add butter and vanilla, beat well and pour into individual sherbet glasses. Sprinkle with nut meats. Serve cold with whipped cream.

Makes 6 servings.

Maple Surprise

Rice Pudding at its very best.

1 cup rice
2 cups milk or water
1 cup thick cream
3/4 cup maple syrup

Cook rice in milk or water in top of double boiler until soft. Whip the cream, add maple syrup gradually and blend with cooked rice. Place in large bowl or individual dishes and set in refrigerator to cool. Serve with thin cream.

Makes 6 servings.

Indian Pudding

Cook 3/4 cup Maltex Cereal or corn meal in 2 cups of boiling water. When thoroughly cooked, add:

1 cup maple sugar
1 cup milk
1/2 teaspoon salt
2 tablespoons melted margarine or butter
2 beaten eggs
1 cup chopped raisins (optional)
1 teaspoon vanilla
Cinnamon and clove to taste

Mix all ingredients together, put in a buttered baking dish and bake 1 hour in oven at 350°F. Serve with thin cream or vanilla ice cream.

Serves 6 people.

Maple Bread Pudding

7 slices bread
3 cups milk, scalded
2/3 cup maple syrup
2 eggs, well beaten
1 teaspoon salt
1 teaspoon cinnamon
1/2 cup raisins

Break bread in pieces in buttered baking dish and pour scalded milk over it. Mix in the remaining ingredients and bake 1 hour in moderate oven (350°F). Serve hot with thin cream or whipped cream.

Serves 8 people.

Maple Spanish Cream

1 tablespoon gelatine
1/4 cup cold water
2 eggs, separated
1/2 cup maple sugar
1 1/2 cups milk
1/4 teaspoon salt
1 teaspoon vanilla

Soak gelatine in cold water. Beat egg yolks; add maple sugar, milk and salt. Cook in top of double boiler until it thickens, slightly. Add gelatine and stir until it dissolves. When cool, fold in stiffly beaten egg whites and vanilla and put in custard cups to chill. Serve with whipped cream.

Makes 6 servings.

Maple Nut Tapioca

2 cups milk
1 cup maple syrup
1/3 cup minute tapioca
1/2 teaspoon salt
1 egg, separated
1/2 cup walnut meats

Scald milk in double boiler; add maple syrup, tapioca and salt. Cook until tapioca is clear, then add beaten egg yolk and cool. Fold in stiffly beaten egg white and chopped nut meats. Serve in sherbet glasses with whipped cream topping.

Makes 6 servings.

Baked Apples

8 tart apples
1 cup soft maple sugar
1 1/2 cups boiling water

Pare and core apples and place in a shallow baking
dish. Fill the center of the apples with soft maple
sugar allowing 2 tablespoons sugar for each apple.
Put water in bottom of dish and bake in moderate
oven (325°F) for 60-90 minutes until apples are
soft, basting frequently with syrup made by melting
sugar and the water. Serve warm with thin cream
poured over the top.

Serves 8 people.

Sponge Cake Sandwich Dessert

An easy dessert, always popular.

2 eight-inch sponge cake layers
1 cup thick cream
1 cup shaved maple sugar
1/4 cup sugar
1 cup chopped butternut meats
1/2 teaspoon vanilla

Mix crushed maple sugar with nut meats and 4 tablespoons of the cream. Spread this on one of the sponge layers as filling and place other layer on top. Whip remaining cream, add sugar and vanilla and spread on top layer.

Serves 8 people.

Maple Ice Cream

1 cup maple syrup
1 cup milk
2 egg yolks
1 pint cream
1 teaspoon vanilla

Boil maple syrup 5 minutes; add beaten egg yolks and milk, stirring with wire whisk. Cool and then stir into stiffly beaten cream. Add vanilla and freeze.

Makes 6 servings.

Maple Baked Peaches

4 large peaches
1/2 cup maple syrup

Peel peaches and cut in halves. Place in glass baking dish, add syrup. Bake in 350°F oven until tender. Serve hot or cold with plain or whipped cream.

Serves 4 people.

Maple Parfait

2 teaspoons gelatine
4 tablespoons cold water
2 eggs, separated
1/2 cup maple syrup
1/4 teaspoon salt
1/2 pint cream
1 teaspoon vanilla

Soak gelatine in cold water and heat in top of double boiler until dissolved. Add egg yolks and beat until light, then add maple syrup. Cook until thick, stirring constantly. Cool and add salt, stiffly beaten egg whites, whipped cream and vanilla. Mix and freeze.

Makes 6 servings.

Fun Fact:
In the U.S., if you see syrup labeled as "maple syrup" that means the syrup has been made almost entirely from maple sap. Only small amounts of other ingredients, such as salt are allowed. Imitation syrups are not even allowed to use the word "maple" in their names.

Maple Torte

1 tablespoon gelatine
1/4 cup cold water
2 eggs, separated
1 cup maple syrup
1/2 teaspoon salt
8 crushed macaroons
3/4 cup chopped nuts
1 cup cream
12 lady fingers

Soak gelatine in cold water. Beat egg yolks slightly, add maple syrup, and cook until thick. Add soaked gelatine and stir until thoroughly dissolved. Cool this mixture, then fold in stiffly-beaten egg whites, crushed macaroons, salt, nuts and whipped cream. Line a mold with lady fingers and pour in the above mixture. Chill and serve with whipped cream or fresh fruit.

Makes 6 servings.

Maple Mousse I

This is a party dessert that will make a hit with your guests.

2 egg yolks
1 pint thick cream
1 cup maple syrup
1 teaspoon vanilla

Place beaten egg yolks and maple syrup in top of double boiler over hot water and cook until mixture thickens, stirring frequently. Let cool, then fold in cream which has been whipped and add vanilla. Freeze in refrigerator tray until firm.

Serves 6 people.

Maple Mousse II

3 eggs
1 pint cream
1 cup maple syrup
1 teaspoon vanilla

Separate eggs, beat yolks into syrup and cook until slightly thick. Cool thoroughly, then fold in whipped cream, stiffly beaten egg whites and vanilla. Freeze until firm, stirring occasionally.

Serves 8 people.

Maple Peanut Mousse

1/4 cup peanut butter
1/2 cup maple syrup
1 1/2 cups thick cream

Stir peanut butter and maple syrup together, using wire whisk, until of smooth consistency. Add whipped cream and pour into freezing tray, stirring occasionally during freezing.

Makes 6 servings.

Icings & Sauces

Maple Icing

3/4 cup maple syrup
1/2 cup sugar
1 egg white
1 teaspoon vanilla

Boil syrup and sugar until it threads when dropped from the tip of a spoon. Pour slowly into stiffly beaten egg white, beating constantly until it holds its shape. Add vanilla and spread quickly over 8-inch square cake.

Maple Sour Cream Frosting

1 1/2 cups maple sugar
3/4 cup sour cream
1/2 cup butternut meats

Cook sugar and sour cream in saucepan until it forms a soft ball when tried in cold water. Remove from fire, beat until creamy and add butternut meats. Spread on 9-inch square cake.

Maple Butternut Icing

This is "extra good" on sour cream cake but is also fine for any white cake.

1 cup sugar
1 cup maple syrup
1/4 teaspoon cream of tartar
1/3 cup water
2 egg whites, beaten stiff
2/3 cup chopped butternut meats

Put sugar, maple syrup, cream of tartar and water in pan. Stir until sugar is dissolved and boil until it spins a thread. Pour gradually over stiffly beaten egg whites, beating constantly until thick enough to stand in peaks. Stir in the butternut meats and spread over favorite white layer cake.

This is enough for 2 layers.

Maple Hard Sauce Icing

If you prefer to make an uncooked icing, this is a good one.

1/3 cup butter or margarine
2 cups confectioner's sugar
3 tablespoons maple syrup
2 tablespoons strong coffee
3 tablespoons cream

Cream butter; add remaining ingredients gradually and alternately. Beat until smooth and creamy. This makes a thick fluffy icing.

Maple Rum Sauce

1 1/2 cups maple syrup
1 tablespoon rum

Cook maple syrup slowly until slightly thick. Add rum and serve on vanilla ice cream.

Foamy Maple Sauce

Wonderful with steamed pudding or gingerbread.

1/4 cup butter
1 cup confectioner's sugar
1 egg, separated
1/4 cup maple syrup
1/4 cup thick cream
1 teaspoon vanilla or maple flavoring

Cream butter; add sugar, egg yolk and maple syrup. Beat until creamy. Fold in stiffly beaten egg white and whipped cream and flavoring.

Maple Sugar Pudding Sauce

1 cup maple sugar
3 tablespoons butter
1 tablespoon flour
1 egg, well beaten
2/3 cup hot water
1 teaspoon vanilla

Mix sugar and flour, stir water in gradually. Let this mixture come to a rolling boil. Remove from fire and pour over butter and well beaten egg, beating vigorously with a wire whisk. Add vanilla. Serve hot.

Maple Syrup Sauce

For cottage pudding, soft custards or plum pudding.

3/4 cup maple syrup
2 egg whites
1/4 cup water
1/2 cup cream
1 teaspoon lemon juice

Boil maple syrup and water until it will spin a thread. Pour this slowly into the stiffly beaten egg whites. Add cream and lemon juice, beating constantly.

Maple Peanut Butter Sauce

Delicious on vanilla ice cream.

1 cup maple syrup
5 tablespoons peanut butter

Blend peanut butter with maple syrup as it is brought to slow boil in sauce pan. Boil gently about 2 minutes. Beat and cool.

Candies

Sugared Popcorn

1 cup maple sugar
3 tablespoons water
1 tablespoon butter
3 quarts popped corn

Boil sugar, butter and water in saucepan until it threads. Pour briskly over 3 quarts of popped corn and stir until evenly distributed over the corn. One cup of nut meats may be mixed with corn if desired.

Popcorn Balls

1 1/2 quarts popped corn
1/2 teaspoon salt
1 teaspoon butter
1/2 cup maple syrup
1/4 cup sugar

Sprinkle salt over popped corn. Cook butter, syrup and sugar to 275°F and pour over corn, stirring constantly. Dip hands in cold water and shape into balls.

Makes 12 balls.

Maple Syrup Fudge

Your young fry will like to make this.

2 cups maple syrup
1 tablespoon light corn syrup
3/4 cup thin cream
1 teaspoon vanilla
3/4 cup walnut or butternut meats, coarsely chopped

Combine maple syrup, corn syrup and cream in saucepan and place over low flame. Stir constantly until mixture begins to boil. Continue cooking without stirring until a small amount of syrup forms a soft ball in cold water. Remove from fire and cool to lukewarm. Beat until mixture thickens and loses its gloss. Add vanilla and nuts and pour at once into 8-inch buttered cake pan. When cool cut into squares.

Uncooked Maple Fondant

2 egg whites
1 cup maple syrup
3 cups superfine confectioner's sugar

Beat egg whites until stiff. Beat maple syrup into these and then continue beating, adding confectioner's sugar gradually until thick and creamy. Form into balls and dip in melted bitter chocolate. Place on waxed paper to cool.

Maple Divinity Fudge

2 cups sugar
2 cups maple syrup
2 egg whites
1/2 cup raisins
1/2 cup cherries
1 cup nuts, chopped

Boil sugar and syrup until it threads. Then pour over the stiffly beaten egg whites and beat until thick. Add raisins, cherries, and nuts. Then turn into 12-inch square pan to cool. Cut in squares.

Maple Sugar Fudge

Always a popular Vermont confection.

2 cups white sugar
1 cup maple sugar
2/3 cup milk
1 tablespoon butter
1 teaspoon vanilla
1 cup walnut or butternut meats

Cook sugars and milk in saucepan for 12 minutes after it begins to boil. Remove from flame and add butter and vanilla. Cool slightly, then beat until thick and creamy. Add nut meats and pour into 8-inch buttered cake tin. Cool and cut in squares.

Fun Fact:
"Sugar shacks" or "sugar houses" were built especially for processing maple sap by boiling down.

Maple Sugar Cakes

Those of you who were brought up on farms will re-member old-fashioned maple sugar cakes. Here's how to make them.

2 pounds maple sugar
1/4 teaspoon cream of tartar
1 cup water

Mix sugar, cream of tartar and water in a kettle and boil until it forms a soft ball when dropped in cold water. Set it away until almost cool, then work with wooden paddle until it becomes thick, creamy and cloudy. Pour into muffin tins to about 1/2 inch thickness. When cold, the cakes will drop out when the tins are inverted.

Makes 12 two-inch cakes.

Maple Cream Candy

Our grandmothers made this for church sales.

2 cups maple sugar
1/2 cup thick cream
1 cup whole butternut meats

Boil sugar and cream slowly until it threads. Add butternut meats and beat until creamy. Pour into buttered cake pan and cut in squares.

Puffed Wheat Candy

1 cup maple syrup
1 tablespoon butter
2 cups puffed wheat

Boil syrup until it forms a soft ball in cold water. Remove from fire, add butter, and beat until it thickens slightly. Add puffed wheat which has been crisped in the oven. Mix well and drop by spoonfuls on waxed paper.

Makes about 36 pieces.

Pulled Maple Candy I

Invite the teenagers in for an old-fashioned candy pull.

3 cups sugar
1 cup maple syrup
1/2 cup water
1 tablespoon vinegar
1/4 teaspoon cream of tartar
1 tablespoon butter
1 teaspoon vanilla

Cook sugar, syrup and water until it reaches a full rolling boil. Add vinegar, cream of tartar and butter. Boil until brittle when dropped in cold water. Remove from fire, add vanilla and pour out on buttered platter. When cool, pull until firm, twist and cut into i-inch sticks.

Makes 54 pieces.

Pulled Maple Candy II

2 cups maple syrup
1 cup sugar
1/4 teaspoon soda
1 tablespoon butter

Boil all ingredients together until brittle when dropped in cold water. Remove from fire and cool on buttered platters. When cold, pull and cut in 1-inch pieces.

Makes 48 pieces.

Yankee Pralines

2 cups sugar
2/3 cup milk
1 cup maple syrup
1 1/2 cups pecan meats

Boil sugar, milk and syrup until it forms a soft ball when dropped in cold water. Remove from fire and cool until lukewarm. Beat until creamy, add nut meats and drop from tip of spoon in small mounds on buttered paper.

Makes 2 dozen.

Caramels

1/3 cup brown sugar
1/3 cup sugar
3/4 cup maple syrup
1/2 cup cream
1 tablespoon butter
1/4 teaspoon salt
1/2 cup nut meats
1 teaspoon vanilla

Cook sugars, syrup and cream together until it forms a firm ball when dropped in cold water. Add remaining ingredients. Without beating, pour into buttered 8-inch pan and chill. Cut in squares and wrap in waxed paper.

Makes 24 caramels.

Main Dishes

Baked Ham Slice

1 1/2 inch center slice ham
1/2 cup maple syrup
1/2 cup dried bread crumbs
1 teaspoon prepared mustard
1/4 teaspoon powdered clove
2 cups milk

Place ham in baking dish and cover top with mixture made with syrup, bread crumbs, mustard and clove. Pour milk around (not over) the ham. Bake slowly (325°F) for 1 1/2 hours.

Serves 4-6 people.

Baked Sliced Ham with Pineapple

1 1/2 inch center slice ham
1/2 cup maple sugar
1/2 cup pineapple juice
1 teaspoon prepared mustard
1 cup pineapple sections

Spread ham with mixture made from maple sugar, mustard, pineapple juice and sections. Bake slowly, 325°F, for 1 1/2 hours.

Serves 4-6 people.

Country Baked Ham

8 pound ham
3 quarts sweet cider
2 cups raisins
2 cups maple sugar
2 teaspoons dry mustard
1 teaspoon powdered cloves
1/2 cup water

Simmer ham in cider for 2 hours. Drain, skin ham and cover it with paste made from maple sugar, mustard, cloves, and water. Place in baking pan, pour cider liquor over it, add raisins to pan, and bake 2 1/2 hours at 325°F. Baste frequently. Make thickened gravy of cider raisin drippings.

Serves 16 people.

Vermont Treat

This is a satisfying one-dish menu for breakfast or luncheon. It includes 4 good Vermont products.

3 cups cooked Maltex Cereal
1 1/2 pounds link sausages
3 large apples
Maple Syrup

Pack cooked Maltex Cereal in loaf pan and cool. When firm, slice and dip in uncooked Maltex Cereal. Fry sliced cereal loaf, sausages and sections of apples in sausage fat. Arrange on platter and garnish with parsley. Pour maple syrup over the fried Maltex Cereal.

This serves 6.

Candied Sweet Potatoes

Cook six medium-sized sweet potatoes until tender. Peel and slice lengthwise. Cover with 3/4 cup maple syrup and dot with butter. Add 1/4 cup water and salt and pepper. Bake about 35 minutes at 350°F.

Makes 6 servings.

Glazed Carrots

Prepare and cook carrots same as candied sweet potatoes.

Baked Sweet Potatoes with Apples

3 large apples
2 tablespoons butter
3 large boiled sweet potatoes
1 teaspoon salt
1/2 cup maple syrup

Core, pare and slice apples and fry in butter until light brown. Slice potatoes. Arrange apples and potatoes in alternate layers in buttered baking dish. Add salt. Pour the syrup over this and dot with butter. Bake in moderate oven (350°F) about 35 minutes.

Makes 6 servings.

Fun Fact:
An average maple tree may produce 9 to 13 gallons of sap per sugaring season.

Country Style Baked Beans

2 cups yellow-eye beans
1/2 pound salt pork, with rind
2 teaspoons salt
1/4 teaspoon powdered mustard
1/2 cup maple syrup
Boiling water

Wash and pick over beans. Soak all night in water to cover. In the morning boil in salted water until tender, about 20 minutes. Drain. Score pork and place half of the pork in bottom of bean pot, rind down. Cover with beans, add mustard and syrup. Place remaining pork on top and fill pot to top with boiling water. Bake in slow oven at 325°F for 4 hours with cover on. Remove cover and put back 1/2 hour more to brown beans and pork.

Makes 6 servings.

Quick Baked Beans

1 quart can yellow-eye beans
1/2 cup maple syrup
1/4 cup chili sauce
1 teaspoon salt
4 strips bacon

Add syrup, chili sauce, and salt to beans. Place in buttered baking dish with bacon slices across the top. Bake at 350°F for 40 minutes.

Serves 4 people.

Baked Bananas

6 bananas
1/2 cup maple syrup
Juice of 1 lemon
1/2 cup crushed cornflakes
1 tablespoon butter

Slice bananas in halves lengthwise and arrange in buttered baking dish. Pour lemon juice mixed with syrup over them. Top with crushed cornflakes and dot with butter. Bake 30 minutes at 350°F.

Makes 6 servings.

Miscellaneous

Mince Meat

This is an original old Vermont maple mincemeat recipe. It was often canned, frozen, or kept in tightly covered stone crocks in very cold cellars.

1 quart chopped beef
1/2 pound chopped suet
1 cup butter
1 pint molasses
2 quarts chopped apples
2 cups seedless raisins
2 pounds maple sugar
1 tablespoon each of cloves, allspice, and cinnamon
2 quarts sweet cider

Mix thoroughly and let boil very slowly in large iron kettle for 2 or 3 hours, stirring frequently to prevent burning.

Sweet Pickles

6 pounds ripe cucumbers
1 quart vinegar
1 teaspoon ground allspice
1 tablespoon ground cinnamon
1 teaspoon ground cloves
3 pounds maple sugar

Peel cucumbers and cut in quarters length-wise. Soak several hours in salted water. Drain and cook slowly until tender in syrup made from vinegar, spices, and maple sugar. Store in stone crock or seal in glass jars.

Maple Sandwiches

Vermont school children like these in their school lunch boxes.

1 cup soft maple sugar
1 cup chopped nut meats
3 tablespoons cream

Blend together and use as filling in whole wheat sandwiches.

Maple Salad Dressing

Good for fruit salads.

1 tablespoon flour
1/4 cup lemon juice
1/2 teaspoon salt
1/2 cup maple syrup
1 cup cream

Blend flour, lemon juice and salt and stir into cold maple syrup. Cook, stirring constantly, until it thickens. Chill, then fold into whipped cream.

Maple Toast

Favorite Sunday breakfast.

8 slices bread
1 cup soft maple sugar
4 tablespoons melted butter

Toast bread to light golden brown. Mix sugar with melted butter and spread on toast. Place in oven or under broiler for 3 minutes.

Serves 4 people 2 slices each.

Whiskey Sour

Use large bar glass.

2 tablespoons maple syrup
Juice of 1/2 lemon
Juice of 1/2 orange
1 1/2 jiggers whiskey
1/4 cup charged water

Mix ingredients and fill glass with shaved ice. Shake well and strain into tall wine glass. Serve with cocktail cherries.

Note: Several of these drink recipes call for charged water. Even doing a search on the Internet I had a hard time coming up with anything but the New Agey type of charged water. Seeing how it is used in recipes I think it is referring to carbonated water or seltzer water. I also saw a recipe that said you could substitute 7-up.

Old Fashioned

Use old fashioned glass.

1 jigger of whiskey
2 dashes of bitters
1 teaspoon maple syrup
1 teaspoon cherry juice

Stir above mixture well. Add 2 ice cubes and decorate with orange slice and cocktail cherry. If too sweet, reduce the maple syrup.

Mint Julep

Use large julep glass.

4 or 5 sprigs of mint, crushed with
2 teaspoons maple syrup
1 dash bitters
2 jiggers whiskey

Fill glass with shaved ice. Stir well. Decorate with lemon slice.

Gin Fizz

1 tablespoon maple syrup
2 ounces gin
Juice of 1/2 lemon
1/2 cup fine ice

Mix syrup, lemon juice and gin. Add ice, stir well.
Strain into tall glass and fill with charged water.

Sherry Flip

1/2 cup chopped ice
1 egg
2 teaspoons maple syrup
1 1/2 wine glass sherry

Shake well, strain into glass and top with grated
nutmeg.

Party Punch

2 1/2 5-ounce cans lemon juice
2 ounces orange bitters
50 ice cubes
1 cup maple syrup
2 quart bottles pale dry ginger ale
3 fifths whiskey

Mix lemon juice, maple syrup, whiskey, bitters and crushed ice cubes. Just before serving, add ginger ale and pour over cake of ice in punch bowl.

Serves 50.

Fun Fact:
In Quebec imitation maple syrup is sometimes referred to as "pole syrup." This joke suggests the syrup has been made by tapping telephone poles. Yummy!

Extras

A maple cookbook would not be complete without recipes for the various foods that just naturally "go with" maple syrup. So here, for your convenience, are some of these standard recipes.

Baking Powder Biscuits

If anyone has failed to know the thrill of hot baking powder biscuits for supper, with the first maple syrup of the season, there's a treat in store for him.

2 cups flour
4 teaspoons baking powder
1 teaspoon salt
2 tablespoons shortening
3/4 cup milk

Mix and sift dry ingredients, work shortening in with tips of fingers. Add milk. Roll on floured board to 3/4 inch thickness. Cut and bake at 375°F for 15 to 20 minutes.

Makes 18 two-inch biscuits.

Sweet Milk Griddle Cakes

A wonderful breakfast the country over.

1 1/2 cups flour
1 teaspoon salt
2 1/2 teaspoons baking powder
2 eggs
1 1/4 cups milk
1 tablespoon melted butter

Mix and sift the dry ingredients, add beaten eggs, milk and melted butter. Fry on hot greased griddle. Brown on one side until bubbles appear on the un-cooked side. Then turn and brown other side.

Makes 18 griddle cakes.

Serve hot with sausage and maple syrup.

Popovers

A hot popover served in a sauce dish with hot maple syrup over it makes a delicious dessert.

2 eggs
1 cup milk
1 cup flour
1/4 teaspoon salt

Beat eggs, add milk, then flour mixed and sifted with salt. Beat until well blended. Bake in heated greased muffin tins in hot oven, 450°F, for 20 minutes, then reduce the heat to 350°F. Bake 15 minutes more.

Makes 9 popovers.

Waffles

2 cups flour
2 teaspoons baking powder
2 tablespoons sugar
1/2 teaspoon salt
2 eggs, separated
2 cups sweet milk
4 tablespoons melted shortening

Sift all dry ingredients into a bowl. Add yolks to the dry mixture, then add milk and melted shortening and beat well. Beat the whites until stiff and fold into first mixture. Cook in pre-heated waffle iron brushed with melted butter.

Makes 6 waffles.

Serve with maple syrup which has been cooked down to the thickness of molasses.

Sour Milk Griddle Cakes

1 cup flour
1/2 teaspoon soda
1/2 teaspoon salt
1 egg
1 cup sour milk
1 teaspoon melted butter

Mix and sift dry ingredients. Add egg, sour milk and melted butter. Cook same as sweet milk griddle cakes on preceding page.

Makes 12 griddle cakes.

Fun Fact:
A "sugarbush" or "sugarwood" is a maple syrup production farm.

All kinds of doughnuts are good with maple syrup, so here are 6 recipes.

Doughnuts (Sweet Milk)

1 egg
1/2 cup sugar
1/2 cup milk
2 cups flour
2 teaspoons baking powder
1/4 teaspoon salt
2 1/2 tablespoons melted shortening

Beat egg, add sugar, milk, flour mixed and sifted with baking powder and salt, then shortening. Mix well. Roll on floured board to 1/4 inch thickness. Shape with doughnut cutter. Fry in deep fat (370°F). Brown on one side, turn and brown on other side. Drain on brown paper.

Makes 18 doughnuts.

Raised Doughnuts

A little more work to make but worth it.

1 ounce yeast cake
1/4 cup lukewarm water
1 pint scalded milk
1/3 cup shortening
1/2 cup sugar
1 teaspoon salt
6 cups flour
1 egg

Dissolve yeast cake in lukewarm water. Pour scalded milk over shortening, sugar and salt. Cool to lukewarm, add dissolved yeast cake, flour, beaten egg. Let rise in warm place to double in bulk. Roll on floured board and cut with doughnut cutter (or cut in strips and twist). Let stand until nearly doubled in bulk. Fry in deep fat, drain on brown paper.

Makes 36 doughnuts.

Plain Doughnuts

"Plain" means unsweetened.

1 cup sour milk
1 tablespoon cream
3 cups flour
1 teaspoon cream of tartar
1/2 teaspoon soda
1/2 teaspoon salt

Place sour milk and cream in mixing bowl. Add dry ingredients mixed and sifted. Toss on floured board and roll lightly to 3/4 inch thickness. Cut in 1-inch strips and twist. Fry in deep fat and serve hot with maple syrup.

Makes 15 doughnuts.

Maple Doughnuts

1 egg
1 cup maple syrup
1 cup milk
2 tablespoons melted shortening
5 cups flour
1 teaspoon cream of tartar
1/2 teaspoon soda
1/4 teaspoon salt

Beat egg well, add maple syrup, milk and melted shortening. Mix and sift dry ingredients and add to above mixture. Toss on floured board and roll to 1/2 inch thickness. Cut and fry in hot fat. Dip in powdered sugar.

Makes 3 dozen average doughnuts.

Sour Milk Doughnuts I

1 egg
1 3/4 cups flour
1/2 cup sugar
1/2 teaspoon soda
1/2 cup sour milk
1 teaspoon baking powder
1/2 teaspoon salt

Beat egg, add sugar, sour milk, flour, soda, baking powder and salt mixed and sifted together. Roll and fry same as in preceding recipe for Maple Doughnuts.

Makes 18 doughnuts.

Sour Milk Doughnuts II

2 eggs
1/2 cup sugar
1/2 cup maple syrup
1/2 cup sour milk
1/2 teaspoon soda
3 cups flour
1 teaspoon baking powder
1/2 teaspoon ginger
1/4 teaspoon cinnamon
1 teaspoon nutmeg
1 teaspoon salt
2 tablespoons melted shortening

Beat eggs and add sugar and maple syrup. Mix soda in sour milk and add to above mixture. Add flour mixed and sifted with other dry ingredients. Add melted shortening and stir well. Knead gently on floured board, cut and fry in deep fat.

Makes 24 doughnuts.

Fritters

4 cups flour
2 teaspoons baking powder
1/2 teaspoon salt
2 cups milk
1 tablespoon thick cream
3 eggs, well beaten

Mix and sift dry ingredients. Add the milk, cream and the well-beaten eggs and stir well. Drop by heaping teaspoons into deep hot fat and fry until well browned.

Serve with warm maple syrup.

Suggested Uses of Maple Syrup

1. Add a tablespoon of maple syrup to a glass of milk. Children love it.

2. Pour a little maple syrup over your favorite hot cereal - Maltex, Maypo Oat Cereal, Oatmeal, Cream of Wheat or others.

3. Fill the hollowed center of grapefruit with maple syrup. It's delicious.

4. Use maple syrup for sweetening in an egg nog.

5. Cook maple syrup down to consistency of molasses and serve it warm on vanilla or maple nut ice cream, lemon sherbet, rice pudding or plain custards.

We hope you enjoyed this cookbook. If so maybe you could stop by Amazon.com and leave us a review or a good rating. This helps us sell books so we can continue to put out more fine books.

For more great cooking pay us a visit at:
http://ChefShane.com

Made in the USA
Middletown, DE
09 October 2016